ACID RAIN

John Baines

STECK-VAUGHN
LIBRARY

Austin, Texas

Conserving Our World

Acid Rain
Conserving Rain Forests
Waste and Recycling
Conserving the Atmosphere
Protecting Wildlife
The Spread of Deserts

Cover: Acid rain is likely to have contributed to the death of these trees in the northern United States.

Series editor: Sue Hadden
Series designer: Ross George

Published in the United States in 1990 by
Steck-Vaughn, Co. Austin, Texas, a subsidiary of National Education Corporation.

© Copyright 1989 Wayland (Publishers) Ltd.

First published in 1989 by
Wayland (Publishers) Ltd.

Library of Congress Cataloging-in-Publication Data

Baines, John D.
  Acid rain.

  (Conserving our world)
  Summary: Discusses the vast contamination of forests and lakes throughout the world by the acidity in the rainfall.
    1. Acid rain—Environmental aspects—Juvenile literature.   2. Pollution—Juvenile literature.   [1. Acid rain—Environmental aspects.   2. Pollution]   I. Title.
II. Series.
TD195.44.B35   1989   363.73′86   89-21656
  ISBN 0-8114-2385-9

Printed in Italy
Bound in the United States.
1 2 3 4 5 6 7 8 9 0 Sa 94 93 92 91 90

Contents

An encounter with a lifeless lake

Our journey through the Swedish forest was almost over. The Ecobus, which had carried our party of teachers from various countries along the bumpy forest road, came to a halt. We got out and walked through the fir trees to a clearing. Suddenly we were faced by a most beautiful lake. The water was so clear and still that the trees and blue sky were reflected in it perfectly. About 40 feet below the surface, the bottom of the lake was clearly visible—in fact it was more like looking through air than water.

I sat quietly by the lake and marveled at the beauty of nature. Then, slowly, a feeling of unease came over me. It was too quiet and too calm. Why were there no birds swimming on the lake? Where were all the water plants that are normally found growing in lakes like this? Surely there must be some small fish in the lake, or some troublesome tiny flies hovering above the surface? But there was nothing to see at all. Suddenly I realized the truth. Our Swedish host had brought us to an acidified lake that had no life in it because of acid rain. Although at first glance the lake seemed beautiful, it was now an ugly example of what people can do to the environment.

This Canadian scene may look very beautiful but the lake contains little life. The clear water suggests that the lake may be suffering from the effects of acid rain.

In Sweden there are hundreds of acidified lakes like this. The lakes have been harmed mostly by acid rain from other countries, which has been carried over Sweden by the wind. Acid rain is caused by burning fossil fuels like coal and oil and allowing them to pollute the atmosphere. This form of pollution is so strong that many trees and lakes are dying, buildings are decaying and, in some cases, people's health is being endangered.

Acid rain is one of many pressures on our environment caused by the modern way of life enjoyed by people in the more industrialized countries. Modern technology has made many people richer, more healthy, and more comfortable than ever before. However, all these benefits depend on our environment, which provides us with everything we need–the air we

Rainwater is not always as pure as it looks. When acid raindrops fall on trees or into lakes, they can cause a build up of acidity, which leads to serious problems.

breathe, the water we drink, the food we eat, the house in which we live, and the school in which we learn. If we continue to damage the environment, then it will not be able to support us as well.

In the following chapters, we will learn more about acid rain and how it can damage the environment. We will also look at the ways in which this problem is being tackled, and ask what we all can do to make sure that the world remains a pleasant place in which to live. After all, it is the only one we have.

Few people in North America or Europe have not heard of "acid rain." The words are used frequently in the press and on television. Acid rain is widely recognized as a cause of serious environmental problems, especially in forests and lakes. The term is used because it is a very dramatic and simple way of describing a very complicated problem. Environmental groups generally talk of "acid precipitation," which includes snow, mist and hail, as well as rain.

How acid is rainwater?

When water evaporates from the ocean, lakes, or the land, the moisture is neither acid nor alkaline. It is neutral. However, the moisture absorbs gases like carbon dioxide found in the atmosphere, and becomes a weak acid. Natural rainfall has a pH of between 5 and 6 (neutral is pH 7). Normal rain can dissolve rocks and create spectacular limestone caves, gorges, and pinnacles, in a process that takes thousands of years.

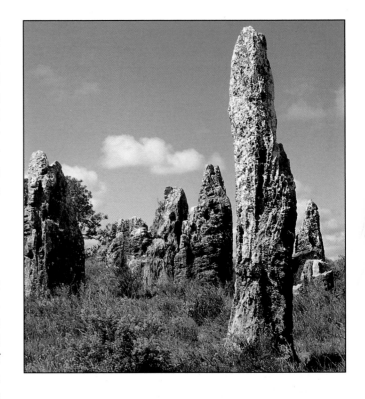

Rain can dissolve limestone into strange shapes, such as these Australian pinnacles.

The Water Pollution Cycle

sulfur dioxide

nitrogen oxides

acid rain

wet deposition

dry deposition

Acids and Alkalis are Opposites

Normally we think of acids in their strong forms when they can be very dangerous. However, they can be neutralized until they are no more acid than lemon juice, vinegar, or a drink of cola.

Alkalis are the opposite of acids, although in their concentrated form, they too can cause damage. Old wooden furniture is often placed in a bath of caustic soda to remove layers of paint and reveal the natural wood beneath. Less powerful alkalis are used in the home regularly including laundry detergent and baking soda.

If you add an acid to an alkali, the concentration of both is reduced. By carefully controlling the amounts added, it is possible for a mixture to become neither acid nor alkaline, but neutral.

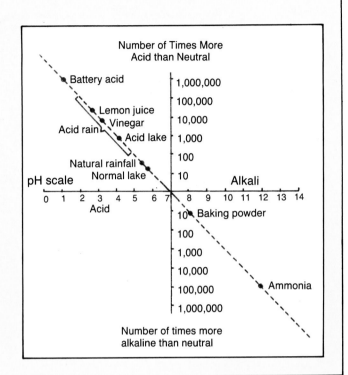

Measuring Acidity

There is a scale for describing the strength of an acid or alkaline solution. It is called the pH scale. The scale extends from zero (very acid) to fourteen (alkaline). The neutral point is seven. Remember, therefore, when pH values are given in this book, that pH 4.5 is more acidic than pH 5.

The pH scale is a logarithmic one. If there are 3 samples, **A** with a pH of 6.5, **B** 5.5, and **C** 4.5, then **B** is ten times more acid than **A**, **C** is 100 times more acid than **A** and 10 times more acid than **B**. An increase in acidity by one unit really means an increase ten times in acidity.

There are various ways of measuring acidity. A cheap way is to use litmus papers—narrow strips of colored paper. When dipped into a solution, the paper turns either red, for acids, or blue, for alkalis. By using the Universal Indicator Scale (shown below), you can determine the pH of the sample.

Natural events can increase the acidity of rainfall. When volcanoes erupt explosively, they release many gases into the atmosphere. Some of these are absorbed by the moisture in the atmosphere and fall as acid rain, but their impact is usually only short-lived.

Air pollution

Most air pollution is caused as a result of burning fossil fuels like coal and oil. These fuels have been formed over thousands of years from dead plants

Above *The spectacular sight of Mount Augustine erupting in Alaska. When volcanoes erupt, they pour many gases into the air, including sulfur dioxide. However, natural events like these only cause about ten percent of air pollution–the rest is caused by human activities.*

Right *Power stations, like this one in Maryland, burn fossil fuel to produce energy. Many gases are released into the atmosphere, some of which cause acid rain.*

Making "Acid Rain"

Put some distilled water in a jar and measure its pH value with litmus paper. Light four matches carefully and put them into the jar of water, keeping the lid slightly open. Let the matches extinguish and then remove them from the jar, closing the lid. Shake the jar so that the water thoroughly absorbs the fumes from the matches. When inserted in the water the paper should now turn reddish-orange because the water has become acidified.

Add some crushed chalk to the solution and shake again. The paper should turn bluish-green because the alkaline chalk will overcome the acid solution.

This experiment simulates acid rain because the burning matches produce sulfur and phosphorous, which are also emitted from chimney smoke. When the gases mix with rainwater it becomes acid rain.

indicates acidity

indicates alkalinity

and animals. Deposits built up and were eventually covered by other rocks and compressed. They remained almost untouched until the middle of the eighteenth century. Since then they have been used in ever-increasing amounts to power cars, heat buildings, and smelt metals such as iron.

When the fuel is burned, not only is the energy released, but many other chemicals are released as well, including sulfur and nitrogen that the organic material contained. These substances are two of the most important ingredients of acid rain. Sulfur and nitrogen are unwanted by-products from the burning of fuels, and so generally they are discharged directly into the atmosphere where they disperse safely, or so it was thought. We now know this is not the case. They convert rapidly into sulfur dioxide and nitrogen oxides which most people agree damage the environment.

The amounts that are discharged into the atmosphere are astonishing: around 24 million tons of sulfur dioxide a year in North America and 44 million tons in Europe. That is enough to fill about 150 supertankers! Most of the sulfur comes from factories and power stations generating electricity.

The quantity of nitrogen oxides produced is smaller, but still amounts to 24 million tons in North America and 16 million tons in Western Europe. Emissions from vehicle engines form most of the nitrogen oxides. With Americans registering 177 million cars and driving 1.7 trillion miles in 1987, the problem is likely to become worse unless immediate action is taken.

What happens to air pollution?

Some of the pollution falls to the ground very quickly, before it is absorbed by moisture. It settles on trees, buildings, and lakes, usually in the area where it was produced. This is called "dry deposition." These deposits build up and later combine with rainwater to become acids.

The rest of the pollution can remain in the air for up to a week and is carried long distances by the wind. During this time, the chemicals react with the moisture in the atmosphere and become diluted sulfuric and nitric acids. These chemicals are ready to become acid rain. They also react with other chemicals in the atmosphere to form secondary pollutants. Ozone is one of the most dangerous of these as it damages vegetation.

When acid precipitation falls as snow, the problems for the environment are delayed, but can be much worse eventually. During the winter, the snow collects on the ground, holding on to its acids. In spring, when the snow melts, there is a

During the spring thaw, the acidity of rivers rises. This photograph shows snow melt in British Columbia, Canada.

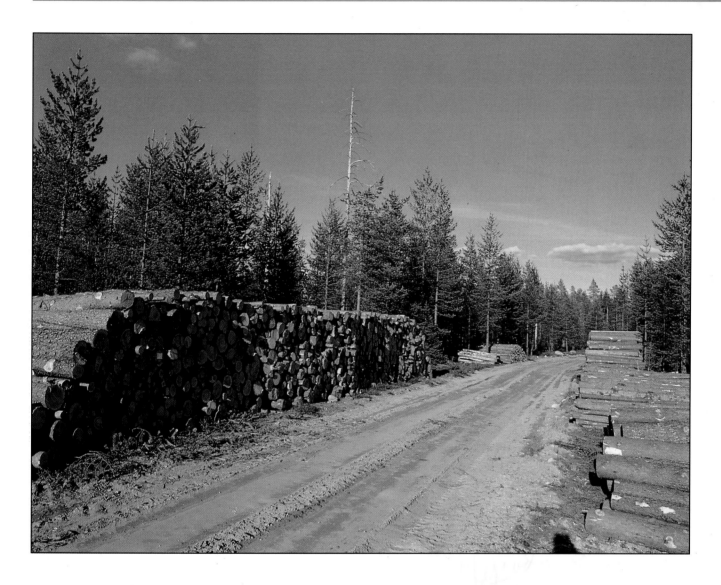

sudden surge of water that flows across the land into streams and lakes. Sometimes a six months' store of acids is released in a few weeks. These "acid surges," as they are called, are particularly harmful to plants and animals.

Farming and forestry

Air pollution is not the only cause of the environment becoming more acidic. As plants grow, they take up and use nutrients from the soil. This increases the acidity of the soil. When the plants die, they rot back into the soil, returning the nutrients and reducing the acidity. Nature has created its own cycle for maintaining

When trees are felled for timber, their nutrients are not returned to the soil. This makes the soil more acid and less able to support future generations of trees. The photograph shows timber piles in Finland, where forestry is an important industry.

stable pH levels. In farming, the plants are removed for food and in forestry the trees are removed for timber. So the nutrients are not returned to the soil to reduce the acidity. To maintain the fertility of the soil, artificial fertilizers are used, especially nitrates. However, these can further increase the acidity of the soil, therefore making the problem even worse.

Air Pollution and the Wind

As long ago as 1661, scientists in Britain found that industrial pollution could affect the health of people and plants in the surrounding area. As industry grew in the eighteenth and nineteenth centuries, damage to people's health and to the environment increased. However, no one thought that the pollution was carried very far. Then in 1881, a Norwegian scientist found what he called "dirty fall-out" on the west coast of Norway where there was no polluting industry. He suspected that it came from Britain. Today scientists have proved beyond doubt that pollution is carried very long distances in the air. If any further proof was needed, then it was provided by the accident at the Soviet nuclear power station, Chernobyl, which led to radioactive rain falling over areas of eastern and western Europe. The effects of this radioactive rain on the environment may last for decades.

Scandinavian countries had recognized that acid rain was one of the chief causes of their lakes becoming acidified. A great deal of research has been undertaken to show the links between sulfur dioxide depositions and environmental damage. Following this evidence, most countries have

Factories like this one in Cumbria, Britain, release smoke into the air, where it is carried long distances by the wind.

agreed to reduce their emissions. Some countries, however, are doing so grudgingly and say that more conclusive evidence is needed to prove that sulfur dioxide causes extensive damage to the environment.

How far can pollution be carried?

If you look at smoke coming from a chimney, there are very few days in the year when it goes straight up. Most often, the smoke bends away from the chimney because the air around the chimney is moving. Even when there appears to be only a slight wind on the ground, higher up it can be much stronger.

The pollution from the chimneys is carried by the wind. Some of it may stay in the air for a week or more before it is deposited on the ground. In that time it can have traveled many miles. Even a gentle wind of 10 miles per hour could carry the pollution about 1,000 miles in five days. The

Acid rain in North America

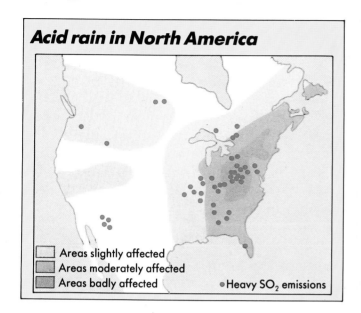

Areas slightly affected
Areas moderately affected
Areas badly affected
● Heavy SO₂ emissions

The above map shows the extent of acid rain fall-out in North America and gives the areas of high sulfur dioxide emissions.

Right *The three diagrams show how sulfur dioxide pollution produced in Europe affects Scandinavia. Diagram 1 shows levels of sulfur dioxide pollution produced in western Europe. Diagram 2 shows how winds carry pollution from Europe to Scandinavia. Diagram 3 shows areas affected by acid rain.*

longer the pollution stays in the atmosphere, the more its chemical composition changes. It becomes a complicated mixture of pollutants that damage the environment.

In the major industrial areas of the northern hemisphere, the prevailing wind (the one that blows most often) is from the west. This means that places downwind of these industrial areas receive the worst pollution. Every year about 3 million tons of acid pollution is blown into Canada from the United States. Of all the sulfur dioxide deposited in eastern Canada, 50 percent comes from the industrial areas of the northeastern United States. In Europe, much of the acid pollution is blown into Scandinavia from Britain and eastern Europe.

How acid rain affects Scandinavia

Diagram 1
Emissions of sulphur

50,000 tonnes/year

50,000 - 200,000 tonnes/year

over 200,000 tonnes/year

Diagram 2

Prevailing wind

Diagram 3

Areas most affected by acid rain

How Acid Rain Affects the Environment

Why is it that in the county of Telemark in southern Norway, some of the lakes are badly affected by acid rain, and some, only a few miles away, are not? Why are the forests close to some industrial areas not as badly damaged by acid rain as those thousands of miles away? The answer lies in the soil.

Soils are formed when rock is broken up by the weather and erosion, and mixed with organic matter from plants and animals. Without soil, most plants cannot grow. The rocks from which the soil is made may be acid, neutral, or alkaline.

Chalk and limestone are rocks that are made from tiny shells that are rich in calcium. Calcium is alkaline and the soils that develop on these rocks are usually alkaline as well. When acid rain falls on alkaline soil, the acid is made weaker, or neutralized, and there are few environmental problems.

Granite is a very hard acidic rock that breaks up very slowly. The soils are usually very thin, but they are able to reduce the acidity of normal rain to a level that plants and animals can tolerate. A balance is maintained. Acid rain overloads this natural system and gradually the environment becomes too acidic for the plants and animals to remain healthy. A new balance is eventually reached, but at a level that cannot support such a rich variety of plants and animals.

Chalk soils support many different plants. Chalk also counteracts acid rain effects.

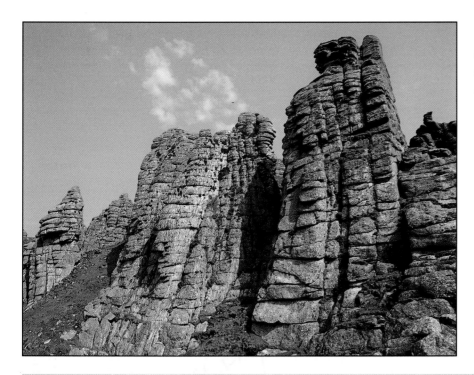

Granite soils can be badly affected by acid rain, so that eventually fewer plants and animals can survive on them.

The Effect of Soils on Acid Rain

Collect a number of soil samples in plastic bags from different areas near your home. Make a funnel from an old plastic bottle by cutting off its bottom. Place a filter paper in the upturned bottle and fill it with soil. Make a solution of water and vinegar with a pH of 4.0. Pour it over the soil sample slowly and collect the water in a beaker as it drips through. Measure its pH value and record it. Repeat the experiment with different soil samples to see how much each one can buffer the acidity of the solution.

Testing soil samples

Animals and plants in areas affected by acid rain have other problems, too. Soils naturally contain small amounts of poisonous minerals like aluminum, cadmium, and mercury. Normally they do not cause serious problems, but as the acidity of the soil increases, chemical reactions allow the minerals to be absorbed by plants. The plants are then damaged and any animals eating them will absorb the poisons, which remain in their body. The harmful minerals are also leached out of the soil into streams and lakes, where they can kill fish and other living creatures. The problems become greater when pollution dumps yet more minerals into the soil. In parts of Poland, vegetable crops have been found to contain ten times more lead than is considered safe.

Acidity in lakes

One of the most popular hobbies in North America and Europe is fishing in lakes and streams. It is enjoyed by millions of people and there is hardly a lake, stream, or river that is not used by anglers. Fishing is also big business. Not only are fishing licenses sold to individuals, but many people are employed in commercial fishing, especially for salmon and trout. Fish farming has become an important economic activity in many remote areas, offering much needed employment to local people. Their livelihood is threatened by acid rain.

About 90 percent of the water in lakes and streams has previously passed through the ground. As the ability of the soil to weaken the acids has fallen, and the acidity of the rainfall has

This Swedish lake has a pH of 5.2, which is harmful to some kinds of fish and other freshwater creatures.

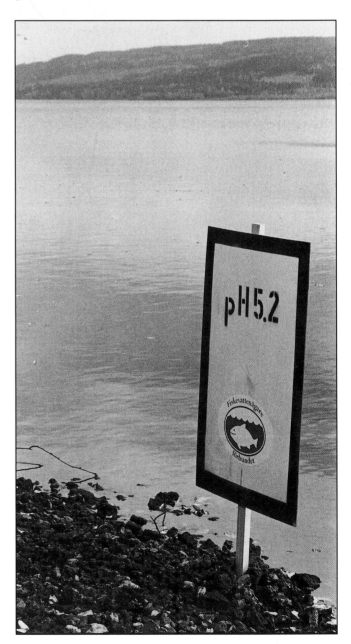

Lake Damage

''There are 14,000 lakes in eastern Canada that have been acidified. You won't find any self-respecting fish swimming around in them . . . another 150,000 now are damaged and 300,000 are threatened.''

Alice Manson

Acid Rain Policy for Environmental Canada

Contaminated Water Supplies

''My family lives in the Swedish countryside and we always used to get our water from a shallow well near the house. My father used to keep a fish in the well to eat any worms that fell into it. We first noticed something was wrong when the fish we put in kept dying. When we measured the pH level, we found that it was 4.9. We also found that the pipes in the house were rotting and we had to replace them all. Some people came to drill a deeper well, but now this has become too acidic also and we have had to install a filter. Fortunately we were able to get a grant from the Swedish government to help pay for it.''

Astrid Fjortoft

A healthy lake teems with wildlife, both above and below the surface. Here a dragonfly rests on a water lily.

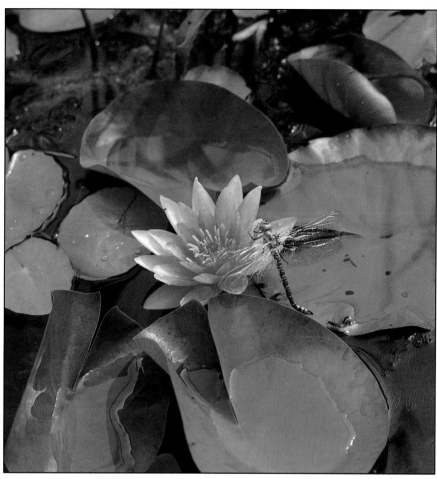

Acidification of Lakes–Some Facts:

- In the southern area of Norway, it is estimated that 90 percent of all trout will have been lost by 1990.

- In the spring thaw of 1984, very acidic water with a pH of 3.8 was recorded in the Vikadel River in Norway.

- Up to 80 percent of the 700,000 lakes in eastern Canada are acid or becoming so.

- Fish have disappeared from more than 200 lakes in the Adirondack Mountains of New York State.

increased, the acidity of the water in the lakes and streams has also increased. Lakes also receive rainfall direct from the sky. There is no chance for the acidity of this water to be reduced by the soil. The situation has become steadily worse in the most sensitive areas of North America and Europe since 1950, although there is evidence that conditions are stabilizing.

A healthy lake has a pH of about 6.5 and is able to support a variety of plants, insects, and fish. In addition, there are a number of animals and birds that feed on the plentiful food in a healthy lake.

The Osprey

The osprey is a large bird of prey that flies low over the surface of a lake and picks fish out of the water with its claws. This spectacular bird is becoming rare in Europe and there is now great concern for its future, as 60 percent of all the breeding pairs in Europe are found in Sweden. If the fish disappear from the Swedish lakes because of acid rain, the osprey too will disappear.

As the pH of the lake falls (the level of acidity rises) the fish find it more difficult to reproduce successfully. Acid levels are highest in spring when the snow melts. This is also the time when the young fish hatch from their eggs. They are unable to tolerate the high levels of acidity and die. It is not only the acid in the water that kills them, but also poisonous minerals such as aluminum that are leached out of the surrounding ground into the water.

The birds that eat these fish also suffer as the harmful minerals become even more concentrated inside their bodies. The shells of their eggs are more fragile and are liable to break, and when the young birds are hatched, their bones may be deformed.

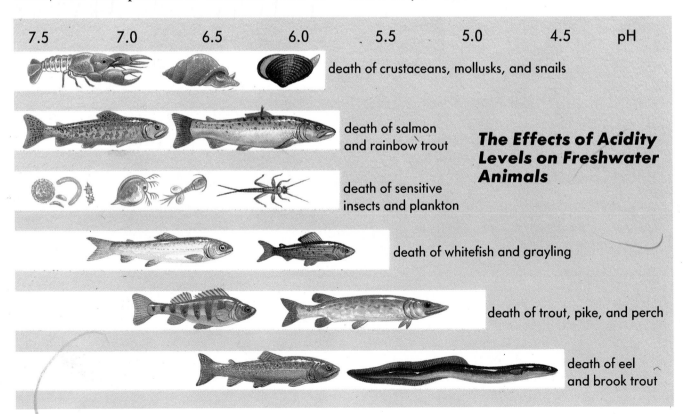

| 7.5 | 7.0 | 6.5 | 6.0 | 5.5 | 5.0 | 4.5 | pH |

death of crustaceans, mollusks, and snails

death of salmon and rainbow trout

The Effects of Acidity Levels on Freshwater Animals

death of sensitive insects and plankton

death of whitefish and grayling

death of trout, pike, and perch

death of eel and brook trout

Acid rain and the seas

The seas were once thought not to be affected by acid rain, but a new report from the Environmental Defense Fund states that acid rain is damaging fish along the Atlantic coast of the United States. Bays and coastal waters that are important fish breeding areas are the worst affected. However, the Reagan Administration remained resolutely opposed to any attempts to curb emissions because, it said, there was not enough evidence of damage. In the report, Dr. Oppenheimer states. "In ignoring the acid rain problem, Congress and the Administration decided to sacrifice thousands of lakes. As it turns out, they were also pulling the plug on our estuaries and coastal waters."

There are reports that acid rain is affecting the Atlantic Coast of the United States. New York and many cities on this coast have certainly suffered from acid rain damage.

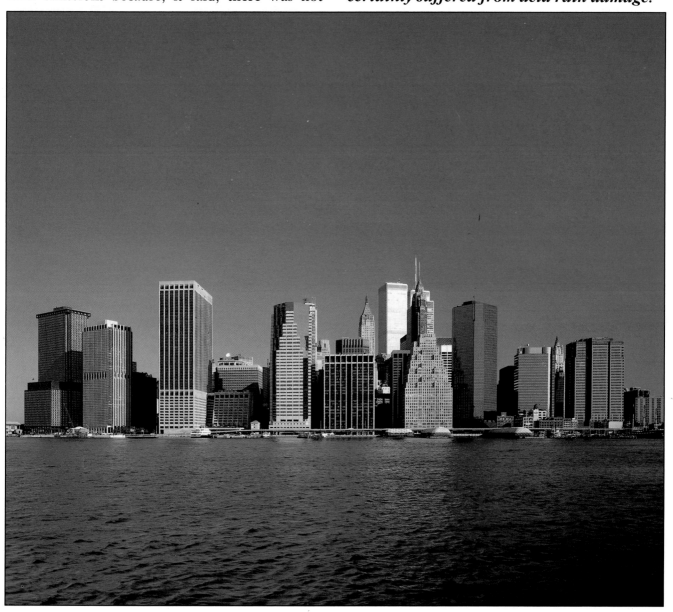

Damage to trees and forests

It was not until the 1960s that acid rain was recognized as a serious threat to forests. The first evidence was found in the Sudetes, a range of mountains important for timber between Poland and Czechoslovakia. Some of the fir trees had very thin branches and others were dying. By the mid 1970s the problems had become much worse and whole stands of trees were dying, while new ones would not grow.

Timber is an important export for Sweden. However, this industry is threatened by acid rain, which has badly damaged many Swedish forests.

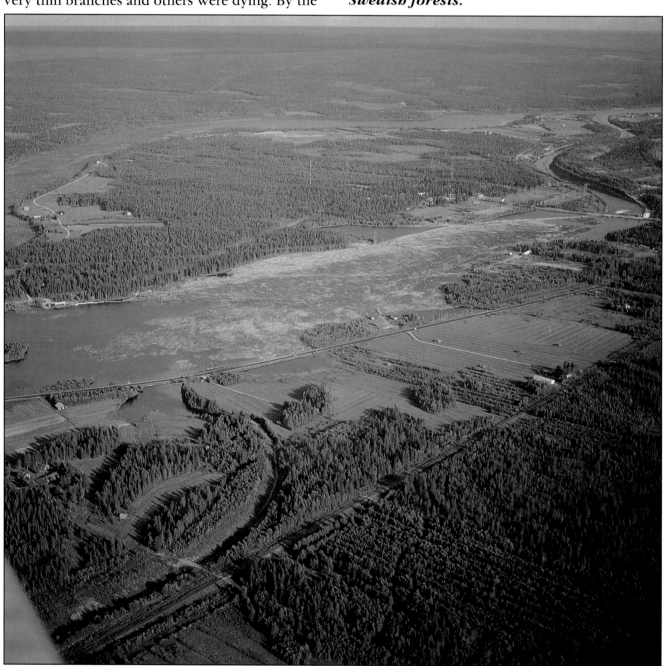

Today, almost 40 percent of the forest is dead or dying. Large areas that were once covered in forest are now desolate. It did not go unnoticed that the Sudetes lie downwind of an industrial area that relies heavily on brown coal (lignite). This releases a lot of sulfur when burned. The use of brown coal had increased from 33 million tons in 1950 to 110 million tons in 1980.

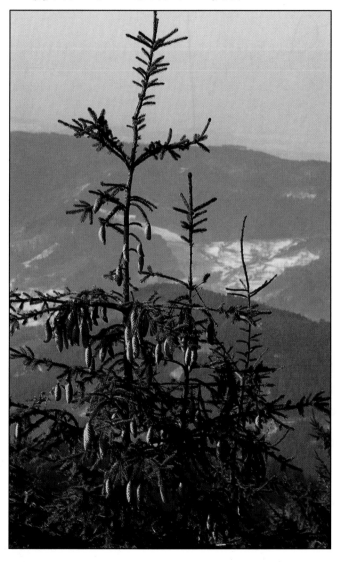

This tree in the German Black Forest is suffering from the effects of acid rain. It is producing many cones, indicating that the tree is close to death and is, therefore, trying to generate new trees.

Seed Growth and Acid Rain

You will need:
Seeds (e.g., clover, peas, mustard, watercress), paper cups, potting soil, vinegar, measuring cup, litmus papers, chalk dust.

Plant each type of seed in its own cup filled 3/4 of an inch from the top with the soil. Use about 12 cups for each type of seed. Water one-third of each group with tap or distilled water, measuring its pH. Water the next third with water and vinegar with a pH level of 4.0, and the last third with water and chalk dust to make the pH about 8.0. Compare the growth of the seedlings over a period of several weeks. Which seeds grew the best?

chalk solution

vinegar solution

distilled water

Not all areas are so badly affected, but there are reports now from all over the world that trees are suffering. A dead tree is easy to recognize, but in most cases death is not due directly to acid rain. Acid rain weakens trees and they may die when blown over or attacked by insects or fungi. Coniferous (evergreen) trees are most at risk, but deciduous (leafed) trees are also affected.

A German scientist displays a branch of a conifer that has lost many of its needles as a result of acid rain.

How Acid Rain Affects Trees

Trees show clear signs of being affected by acid rain. The main symptoms are:

Less foliage: *Coniferous trees do not drop their needles annually like deciduous trees. Foresters are able to recognize needles on a healthy tree that are up to 7 years old. Damaged trees lose needles more quickly and they look very scraggy. Deciduous trees grow less foliage in the summer. One sign of this is that it is possible to see the sky through the tree. These trees also drop their leaves earlier than normal in autumn.*

Yellow spots: *The sulfur dioxide in the atmosphere causes the needles of conifers to develop yellow spots.*

Many cones produced: *A damaged conifer close to death produces a great many cones which are the seeds from which new trees can grow.*

Die-back: *Those parts of the conifer most exposed to acid rain, such as the top and the tips of the branches, lose more needles than the rest of the tree.*

Canadian maple trees, the source of maple syrup, are now being damaged by acid rain.

Forest Damage

"My family has lived on this farm for over 100 years. It covers about 70 acres, 57 of which are forest. Every year a contractor comes in to fell some of the trees. The older trees are over 100 years old and fetch a high price, as they can be used for timber. However, many of these old trees are now damaged by the acid rain and are dying from insect attacks. A couple of years ago a strong wind blew some trees down. The younger trees will never reach this age. The damage from the acid rain becomes so severe when they are over 50 years old, that I have to fell them while they can still be used as timber instead of wood pulp."

Ingemar Zachrisson; Sweden

Ingemar Zachrisson explains about acid rain to visitors.

The damage to buildings

If you look at many buildings, especially old ones, you may well notice that the building materials are breaking up. Building materials weather naturally, but over a long period of time, usually many centuries. Acid rain speeds up the process. In 1984, the Statue of Liberty in New York harbor had to be partially dismantled for restoration because acid pollution had corroded the metal frame and copper covering. Millions of dollars had to be spent to return it to its former glory, but who should pay? Should it be the tax payers of New York or the factories that caused the pollution in the first place?

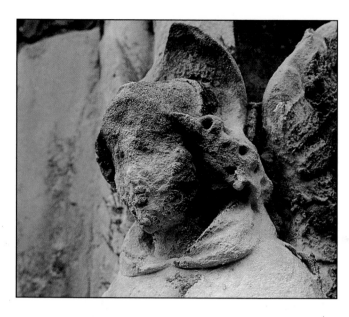

Below *America's most famous landmark, the Statue of Liberty, being restored in 1984.*

Above *The corrosion of this English church statue has been accelerated by acid rain.*

Can acid rain damage your health?

In some areas, breathing "fresh" air carries a health warning, especially for the elderly and those who suffer from asthma or other breathing problems, or have a heart problem. In West Germany, the concentrations of sulfur dioxide in the atmosphere have become so dangerous on occasions that people are advised not to go out. In Los Angeles in 1978, there were 23 days on which some industries had to stop burning coal and oil, while outdoor activities at school had to be

In West Germany's industrial area, the Ruhr, smog can be so serious that traffic detours are necessary.

canceled outright.

However, following legislation to clean up car exhausts (the major source of this particular pollution) the situation has improved. The first year since 1955 that no emergency measures had to be taken was in 1984. Pollution is therefore not an inevitable result of industrial progress. If we control it, we can all enjoy a healthier life.

If, having read this far, you are feeling very concerned about the damage being caused to the environment by acid rain, take some heart from the fact that millions of other people feel like you, in the United States, Britain, Canada, Norway, Sweden, West Germany, and many other countries. They include young and old, factory workers, farmers, industrialists, politicians, writers, scientists...in fact, people from all walks of life. It is only a matter of time before everyone will realize the true extent of this problem.

Two of the countries among the most reluctant to accept that acid rain could cause problems, West Germany and Britain, are both taking steps to reduce pollution. West Germany changed its policy almost overnight when it was found that its own forests were suffering badly. West Germany is now one of the leading countries

Reducing Sulfur Dioxide Levels

Signatories to the Geneva Convention	Reduction from 1980 level		
Austria	70%	by	1995
Canada	50%	by	1994
East Germany	30%	by	1993
France	50%	by	1990
Italy	30%	by	1993
Netherlands	50%	by	1995
Norway	50%	by	1994
Soviet Union	30%	by	1993
Sweden	65%	by	1995
United Kingdom	30%	by	1999
West Germany	65%	by	1993

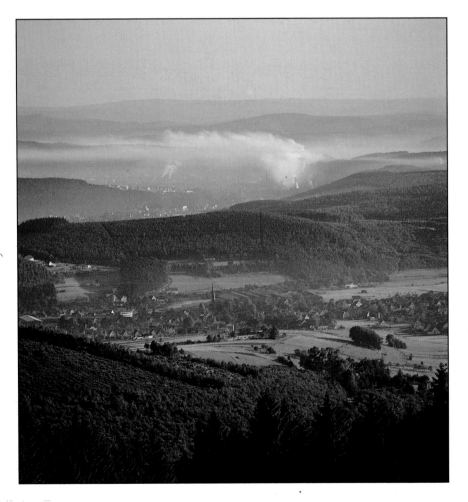

Above *The table lists some of the countries that signed the Economic Commission for Europe's 1985 protocol on air pollution. By doing so, each country agreed to reduce its emissions of sulfur dioxide by at least 30 percent.*

Left *A layer of pollution is trapped over the Hüttental valley in West Germany. When the Germans realized that pollution was harming their much-loved forests, they quickly resolved to take preventive action.*

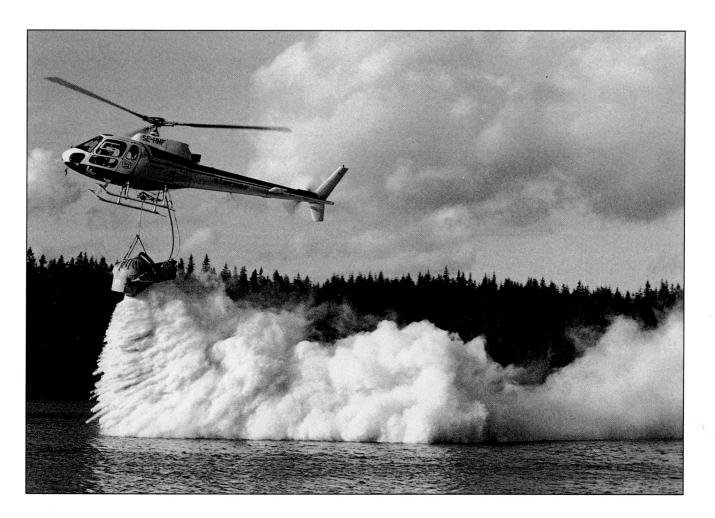

pressing for stricter pollution controls. Britain, which is not facing problems as serious as West Germany, would prefer to wait for more conclusive proof. However, it is under pressure from other European governments to take action. U.S. President George Bush pledged recently to strengthen clean-air legislation and cut emissions that lead to acid rain by 50 percent by 2000.

It will take a long time before all the causes of acid rain are removed. In the meantime, something has to be done to reduce the impact of acid rain on the environment today.

Liming

You have already read that alkalis help neutralize acids. Lime (crushed limestone) is an alkali and is able to reduce the acidity when put in lakes,

A Swedish lake is limed by helicopter.

streams, or on the land. Lime is most frequently used to reduce the acidity of lakes. The amount needed to restore the acidity to a healthy 6.5 pH varies depending upon the size and acidity of the lake. Typically about 1.75 tons per acre will be needed to raise the pH from 5.5 to 6.5. After liming, species of plants and animals are quick to return to the lake. As the toxic metals are carried to the bottom of the lake, fish can breed more successfully. The only species to suffer are those that live at the bottom of the lake where the metals accumulate. To prevent the problems from recurring, liming has to be repeated every two to five years. Maintaining lakes in a healthy condition is therefore time-consuming and very expensive, especially in remote areas.

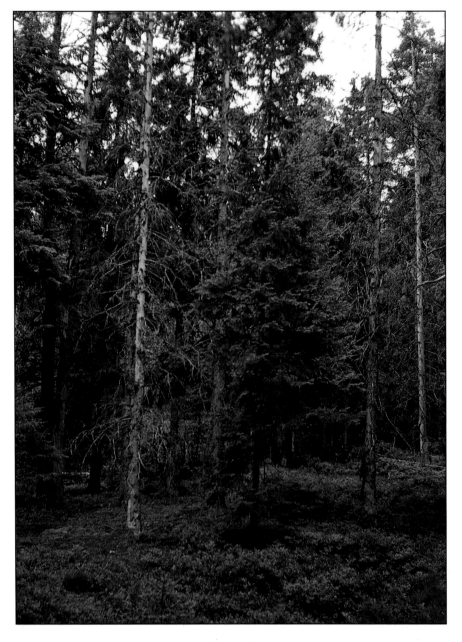

Left *Many trees in Scandinavia have been killed by acid rain. The acidity of the soil can be neutralized with lime, but it is difficult to apply lime in dense forests.*

Right *Power stations provide much of the energy we need for our way of life. Modern methods of energy conservation could reduce fuel consumption by 50 percent while still allowing us to enjoy a high standard of living.*

Different ways of applying the lime are tested. In some areas, lime is released constantly into running water, but this requires the use of expensive machinery. In remote areas lime is dropped into the water by airplane or helicopter. A particularly effective way is spreading the lime over ice-covered lakes in winter. The lime falls into the water when the ice melts in spring–the same time as the acidity increases when all the melt water runs into the lakes. In some areas, lime is spread on the land itself. This is very effective in reducing the acidity of the soil, as well as the water, and is therefore of benefit to the vegetation as well.

The extent of the damage caused by acid rain is so great that liming will never solve the problem. It has been estimated that it would take over 330,000 tons of lime a year at a cost of more than 250 million Norwegian Kroner (about 40 million dollars) to neutralize the acids in southern

Norway alone. Locally, however, the successes have been striking.

There are no technical problems in preventing air pollution. The obstacles that have to be overcome are finding the money and, perhaps more importantly, the desire to put a stop to acid rain. Two courses of action are needed. One is to take the practical action needed to reduce emissions of sulfur dioxide and nitrogen oxides. The other is to reach international agreements to make sure that action is taken.

Listed below are some practical ways of reducing the problem of acid rain. You can play your part in helping to solve this problem.

Conservation of energy

The Western way of life involves using a great deal of energy, for example in transportation, manufacturing products, heating, lighting, and cooking. Yet it has been estimated that if we used the fuel more efficiently and took measures to conserve energy, then we could still enjoy a high standard of living while consuming 50 percent less energy. The less energy is used, the less pollution is produced.

Using alternative sources of energy

Coal, oil, and natural gas are used to produce over 75 percent of the world's energy requirements. These sources will eventually run out. It is possible to use natural sources of energy to generate power that will not run out. These are called renewable sources of energy. They include hydroelectric power (using the power of falling water to drive generators), biomass (burning plant and animal matter), geothermal energy (using natural heat deep in the earth's crust), wave and tidal power from the sea, and wind

Left *The solar energy station at Odeillo, France, harnesses the energy of the sun.*

Below *Windmills are used to generate electricity at this wind farm in California.*

This Swiss hydroelectric power station uses water to generate electricity.

power (from windmills). Nuclear power, which creates energy by splitting atoms, is also renewable and does not produce pollutants such as sulfur dioxide and nitrogen oxides. However, many people fear the dangers of nuclear accidents and are concerned about the disposal of nuclear waste.

Hydroelectric power is one of the best developed of the renewable resources, providing 25 percent of the world's electricity. However, this could be increased dramatically with minimum damage to the environment. At present, wind and wave power receive very little money for research and development. However, the wind farms of California have shown that nonpolluting energy can be produced economically and in quantity.

31

Britain's Drax power station will use a liming process to remove 90 percent of its sulfur dioxide pollution.

Use of low-sulfur fuels

Not all coal and fuel oils contain a lot of sulfur. By switching to these sources, the amount of pollution could be reduced. But what would be the effect on those areas where people mine fuel with a high sulfur content? Would there be a lot of unemployment?

Removing pollution at source

Sulfur can be removed from fuel before it is burned, and sold as a by-product to industry. This would actually improve employment prospects in the mining areas, but only if the coal could still be sold at a high price. Alternatively, the sulfur can be removed from the fumes before they are sent into the atmosphere. This can be done using devices called scrubbers positioned in the chimneys. These scrubbers spray a slurry of limestone into the fumes.

Changing methods of farming and forestry

Farming and forestry can increase the acidity of the soil. If foresters take and use the whole of a tree, including the branches and roots, it is the equivalent of the soil being exposed to acid rain for about 60 years. If only the trunk of a tree is taken, and the rest is left to rot back into the ground, less acidity builds up in the soil.

More and more foresters are leaving the roots and branches of felled trees to rot into the soil. This releases nutrients back into the soil, thus improving its ability to support future forestry plantations.

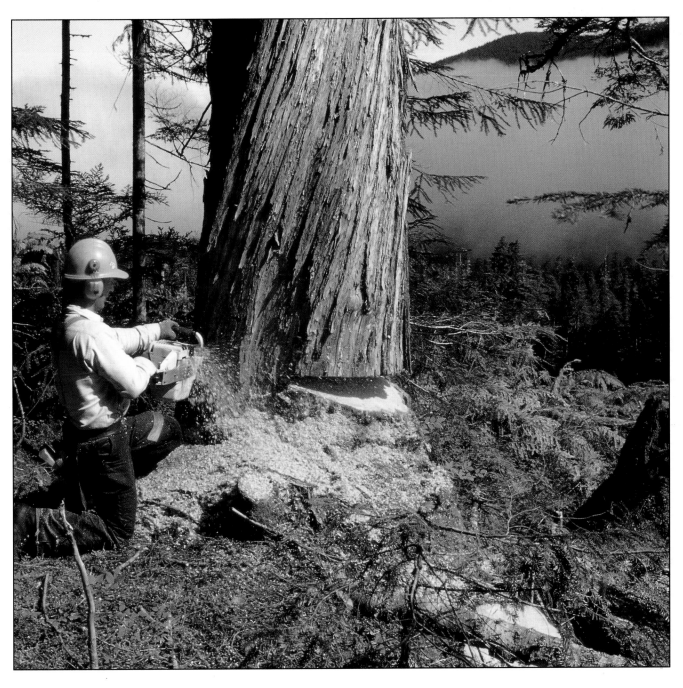

Changing our behavior

There are actions that each one of us can take now to reduce pollution problems. By turning down the central heating thermostat by only a couple of degrees, considerably less fuel is used. We could put on extra clothing when cold, instead of turning up the heat. Driving more slowly reduces the amount of nitrogen oxides produced by car engines. In some countries speed limits could be reduced. A limit of about 55 mph seems to be a good compromise between speed and pollution. A great deal of energy and pollution would be saved if more people regularly used public transportation instead of traveling in their own car.

Traffic jams, such as this one in São Paulo, Brazil, could often be avoided if more people used public transportation.

Cleaning up vehicle exhausts

Vehicle engines produce nitrogen oxides and other pollutants. Car engine exhausts can be cleaned up by using lead-free gasoline and fitting a catalytic converter. These convert 90 percent of the harmful gases in car exhausts into less harmful carbon dioxide, nitrogen, and water vapor. An alternative would be to develop lean-burn engines, which are more efficient and produce less pollution. Diesel engines are cheaper to run because they consume less fuel than gasoline engines. However, they produce more smoke— twice as much nitrogen oxide and six times as much sulfur dioxide.

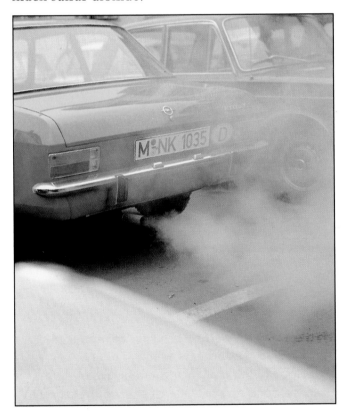

Car exhaust fumes contain carbon monoxide, nitrogen oxides, sulfur dioxide, and hydrocarbons (unburned fuel). A catalytic converter would convert most of these substances into carbon dioxide, nitrogen, and water vapor.

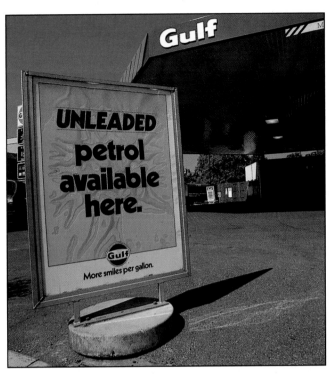

This British sign notes that lead-free gas is a first step toward cleaner car exhausts.

Some countries, such as the United States and Japan, already have strict laws that control pollution from cars. In the 1990s, European regulations will require all cars with engines over two litres to be fitted with catalytic converters. This would dramatically improve the quality of the air. A simple way of avoiding polluting the air is to switch off the car engine when it is not moving. In Switzerland and West Germany, notices at traffic lights instruct drivers to turn off their engines while waiting, rather than allowing them to pour toxic fumes into the air.

Education

Scientists can identify problems and find solutions to them, but unless people in general are aware of the seriousness of the problems, there is little incentive for anyone to take action. Education plays an important part in making people aware of environmental problems.

It costs a lot of money to clean up acid rain. Many countries were reluctant to take action until scientists showed them by how much pollution needs to be cut. Scientists have been doing these calculations for sulfur dioxide and nitrogen oxides and have shown that the more sensitive areas of Norway and Sweden are only capable of absorbing between .01-.017 ounces of sulfur dioxide and .035-.07 ounces of nitrogen oxides over a square yard. Levels in many areas of Scandinavia are much higher than this, for example .07-.1 ounces of sulfur and .07-.1 ounces of nitrogen over a square yard. Scientists estimate that the world as a whole needs to cut down the emissions of these two pollutants by between 80 and 90 percent. This means that every 100 tons currently put into the atmosphere must be reduced to 10 tons in as short a time as possible.

Over the last ten years in Europe, emissions of sulfur dioxide have decreased by about 25 percent. The total amount falling on Scandinavia has dropped by a similar amount and the good news is that some of the lakes are recovering slightly. Many countries are committed to reducing pollution still further and it is estimated that a further drop of 30 percent will be achieved by the mid 1990s.

These results have only been achieved because research has been able to show that pollution damages the environment and that pollution is carried by the wind from one country to another. The research will continue, but at the same time countries, such as the United States and Canada, are working together to try to reduce emissions still further by making agreements controlling pollution with one another.

Members of Greenpeace climbed a German factory chimney to draw attention to the pollution it produces.

Opposite *Members of the European parliament frequently meet together to discuss environmental issues.*

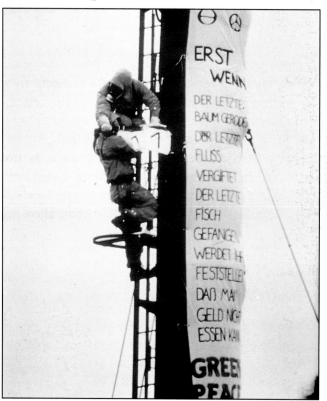

Saving a Swedish lake

''Our lake has been saved by schoolchildren from the city. They came out here on a field trip with their teacher and learned that at one time the lake teemed with wildlife. Then it became acidified, and many species were disappearing. The children wanted to help us save it, so they came back in the winter and helped us spread nine tons of lime on the surface of the ice. That summer, when they came back again, they measured the acidity and found that it had fallen from a pH of 5.7 to a pH of 6.8. They worked very hard, but they seemed to enjoy themselves as well and are very proud of what they have achieved. We could not have done it so quickly without them.''

Björn Hansen

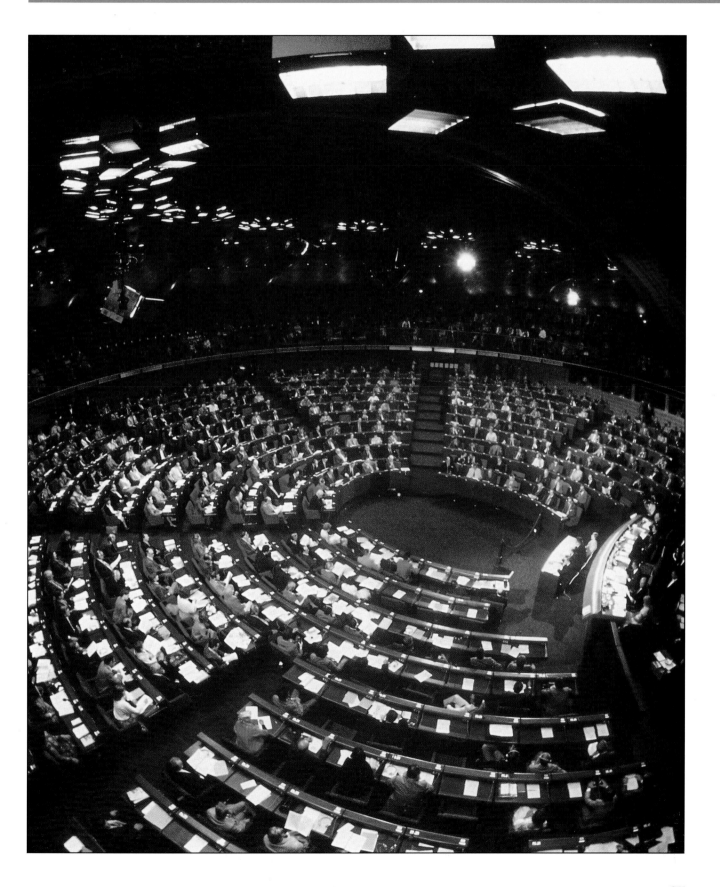

Reducing nitrogen oxides

Sulfur dioxide is only one of the pollutants causing acid rain problems, but it is the one that has been studied the most. Nitrogen oxides are more complex to study, but in 1986 negotiations started on an international agreement to reduce pollution from nitrogen oxides. There have been problems in reaching agreement on how ambitious the targets should be. West Germany has proposed that there should be a 30 percent reduction on 1985 nitrogen oxide levels by 1995. This is supported by a number of countries. Britain and France, however, seem to be willing to

Los Angeles pioneered control of vehicle pollution to solve its smog problems.

go only as far as a "freeze," which means no further increase in emissions. President Bush proposed in 1989 to cut nitrogen oxide emissions by two million tons or about one-tenth a year.

About 50 percent of the nitrogen oxides are present in the air as a result of emissions from vehicles. If the amount of pollutants coming from exhausts is reduced, then the total amount of nitrogen oxides in the air is reduced. The United States and Japan are the furthest advanced with strict laws controlling the level of emissions from car exhausts. American drivers can be stopped, their exhaust tested, and the driver forbidden to continue if the exhaust is not clean enough. Perhaps the positive action taken by the United States and Japan will encourage other countries to introduce stricter controls on exhaust fumes.

International Developments on Emissions of Sulfur Dioxide

1872 The term "acid rain" used for the first time by Robert Smith, Great Britain's first pollution inspector.

1881 Traces of acid rain are noted in Norway.

1921 Some lakes in southern Norway are found to have no fish in them. Research shows that there is a direct link between fish deaths and the levels of acidity in the lakes.

1950 Concern about acid rain spreads to nations beyond Scandinavia including the United States, Canada, Britain, and the Soviet Union.

1970 The United States Clean Air Act leads to the strongest controls in the world to reduce pollution from vehicle exhausts.

1976 OECD (Organization of Economic Cooperation and Development) produces a report stating that pollution produced in one European country is damaging the environment in others. A network of rain sampling stations is set up in Canada to find out more about acid rain.

1977 The United Nations Economic Commission for Europe (ECE) sets up a program to monitor long-range pollution.

1978 The National Atmospheric Detection Program is set up in the United States to find out more about pollution in the atmosphere.

1979 Over 30 countries sign an ECE convention agreeing to reduce atmospheric pollution. However, the wording is very weak because West Germany and Britain do not want controls. The wording they eventually agree to is to "endeavor to limit and so far as possible gradually reduce and prevent air pollution using the best available technology that is economically feasible." In other words, if they do not want to do anything, they could always say it would be too expensive.

1980 The United States and Canada sign a declaration of intent to prevent pollution from damaging each other's countries.

1981 OECD publishes a report showing that it would be cheaper to reduce sulfur emissions than to let environment damage continue.

1982 Canada offers to reduce sulfur dioxide emissions by 50 percent if the United States will do the same. The United States refuses.

1983 West German scientists draw international attention to the link between forest damage and acid rain.

1985 A total of 19 countries sign a protocol within the ECE convention and agree to cut sulfur dioxide emissions by 30 percent. This group became known as "The 30 percent Club." The U.S., Poland, and Britain do not sign and there are not enough signatories for it to come into effect.

1987 Sufficient countries sign the 30 percent protocol for it to come into effect. The United States and Britain still do not sign.

1988 End of European Year of the Environment coincides with the European Economic Community's failure to agree on plans to cut further the emissions of sulfur dioxide from power stations.

1989 U.S. President Bush proposes stronger measures for Clean Air Act.

What Can We Learn From Acid Rain?

In this book we have seen much evidence that acid rain can damage the environment. But we have also learned many other things about the environment and ourselves. These will help you when you come to look at other environmental issues.

We have learned that not everyone agrees about the causes of environmental damage or the solutions needed. Some say there is still not enough evidence that acid rain damages the environment. Based upon the information you can collect from other sources, you will have to make up your own mind. Before you reach conclusions about any environmental issue, you should consider all the evidence available for each point of view.

You have also learned that, left to themselves, plants and animals achieve an ecological balance. From one year to the next, the environment of the wood, the lake, the marsh, or the desert does not change very much. Many species, including humans, live and depend on one another in these environments. Yet we are the only species that has the ability to change the environment significantly. Sometimes our activities upset the balance so much that the environment is damaged. However, we can also work with nature to protect the environment, while still using it to meet our many needs.

Sometimes the evidence that pollution harms the environment is hard to deny.

An electronic billboard in a Tokyo street displays levels of noise and air pollution.

It is people who finally determine the kind of environment in which we have to live. We all share the responsibility to care for our planet. It is easy to blame others for creating an environment we do not like but have we damaged it by our own actions? Think about this and decide if you would like to do something to protect our environment. You can help by saving energy, as suggested in a previous chapter, or you may like to join an environmental organization. Some useful addresses are listed at the back of this book, and your teacher will also be able to give you some advice.

A cleaner environment means cleaner cities and healthy trees and lakes for all to enjoy.

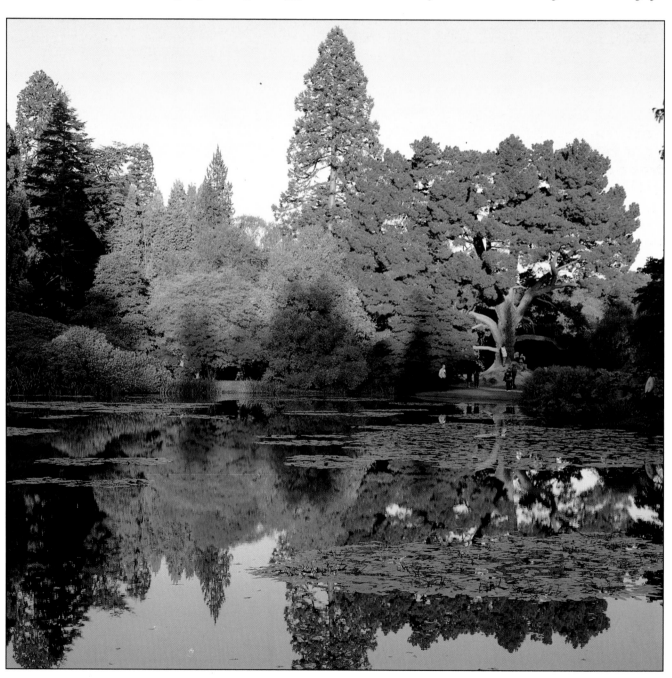

Glossary

Acid A solution with a pH value of less than 7.0. It is capable of neutralizing an alkali.

Alkali A solution capable of neutralizing an acid. It has a pH value greater than 7.0.

Atmosphere The gaseous layer that surrounds the earth. Not counting water vapor, it consists of nitrogen (78 percent), oxygen (21 percent), argon (1 percent) and very tiny amounts of carbon dioxide, neon, ozone, hydrogen, krypton, and pollutants. Water vapor generally represents between 1 and 4 percent of the atmosphere.

Brown coal (lignite) Dead vegetation that has not been fully compressed to become coal.

Buffer The ability of soils and water to neutralize or partly neutralize acid precipitation.

Catalytic converter A device placed on car exhausts to remove pollution.

Convention An agreement made by a group of countries to work together toward a common goal.

Ecosystem A community of plants and animals and the environment in which they live.

Emissions Substances discharged into the air from chimneys and vehicle exhausts.

Environment A plant's or animal's surroundings, including the air, water, soil, and rock types.

Fossil fuels Fuels derived from organic substances, for example, coal, oil, and natural gas.

Heavy metals Metals like cadmium, aluminum, and mercury, which are found in the soil and are poisonous to plants and animals.

Leaching The process by which water moves minerals from one layer of soil to another, or into streams.

Liming Dumping alkaline substances, such as crushed limestone, into waterways, lakes, or onto the ground to neutralize high levels of acidity.

Neutralize To reduce the level of acidity in a substance, so that it becomes neither acid nor alkaline (pH 7).

Nitrogen oxides (NOx) Gases formed mainly from nitrogen in the atmosphere when fuels are burned at a high temperature.

Organic material Matter that is living or was once living.

Organism Any animal or plant that can sustain life by itself.

Ozone A form of oxygen that can damage plant growth and irritate the eyes and breathing system. However, ozone forms a vital layer of the atmosphere, shielding the earth from the sun's harmful ultraviolet rays.

pH The unit for measuring acidity.

Pollutants Substances that can damage the air, water, or the land when released into it.

Pollution The presence of harmful substances in the environment.

Precipitation Moisture that falls to the earth such as rain, sleet, snow, or mist.

Prevailing wind The direction from which the wind most often blows.

Protocol An agreement that is part of a convention.

Scrubber A device attached to a chimney that sprays a liquid through the gases to remove pollutants like sulfur dioxide.

Sulfur dioxide (SO2) A strong-smelling, colorless gas formed mainly from the burning of fossil fuels.

Toxic Harmful or poisonous.

United Nations The international organization that brings all the countries of the world together to discuss, and attempt to solve, world problems.

Further Reading

Pamphlets

Acid Rain

United States Environmental Protection Agency, Washington, D.C. 20460
Acid precipitation is defined as one of the major environmental problems of the decade. Contains facts, history, effects, factors—black and white photographs, charts, diagrams, further reading list—36 pages. Copies may be obtained by writing to:

Publications
Center for Environmental Research
Information
US EPA
Cincinnati, Ohio 45268

Acid Rain: Effects on Fish and Wildlife

United States Department of the Interior, 1985
Kathleen Stecker Mayer and Ell-Piret Multer
Government leaflet on the effects of acid rain on fish and wildlife. Charts, maps, list of supplemental information. Copies may be obtained from:

Publications Unit
U.S. Fish and Wildlife Service
Washington, D.C. 20240

The Acid Rain Story

Ministry of Supply and Services Canada, 1984
A 15-page pamphlet describing acid rain, its effects on the environment, alternate forms of non-acid producing energy, and international efforts to reduce emissions—color photographs, maps, illustrations. For additional information:

Information Directorate
Environment Canada
Ottawa, Ontario K1A OH3

Acid Rain: The Controversy

Dr. Arnold and Connie Krochmal
Pamphlet Publications Publishing
PO Box 335
Dayton, OH 45459
An overview of acid rain, components, factors, effects, damage, emissions, etc. Lists periodical articles.

Downwind: The Acid Rain Story

Minister of Supply and Services Canada, 1982
Pamphlet gives overview of the acid rain situation. Color photographs, maps, charts, and additional reading list. For additional information:

Information Directorate
Environment Canada
Ottawa, Ontario K1A OH3

How Harmful is Acid Rain

Greenhaven Press, Inc., 1986
577 Shoreview Park Road
St. Paul, Minnesota 55126
This pamphlet is chapter six from *The Environmental Crisis: Opposing Viewpoints.* Intended to confront the reader with various points of view. Offers an additional reading list.

Water Fact Sheet: Acid Rain

Sheet containing water facts on acid rain, pH scale—1984. For further information on technical and overview reports, and hydrologic data contact:

Hydrologic Information Unit
U.S. Geological Survey
419 National Center
Reston, Virginia 22092

Books

A Killing Rain
The Global Threat of Acid Precipitation
Thomas Pawlick
(Sierra Club Books, 1984)
Acid rain versus administrators and lawmakers.

Acid Rain
Robert H. Boyle and R. Alexander Boyle
(Nick Lyons Books, 1983)
The scope of the problem to the political stall
to the solution.

Troubled Skies, Troubled Waters
The Story of Acid Rain
Jon R. Luoma
(Viking Press, 1984)
The origins and effects of acid precipitation
and the political tangle.

Who's Poisoning America?
Corporate Polluters and their Victims in the
Chemical Age
Edited by Ralph Nader, Ronald Brownstein,
John Richard
(Sierra Club Books, 1981)
Seven case studies of chemical pollution.

Useful Addresses

The Acid Rain Foundation
1630 Blackhawk Hills
St. Paul, Minn. 55122

Aims to develop and raise public awareness of
the issue and supplies educational resources.

Acid Rain Information Clearing House
Center for Environmental Information, Inc.
33 S. Washington Street
Rochester, N.Y. 14608

Provides general information about acid rain.

Children of the Green Earth
PO Box 95219
Seattle, Wash. 98145

Promotes and organizes children's tree planting
projects and various educational activities.
Publications.

Conservation Foundation
1250 24th Street N.W.
Washington, D.C. 20037

Promotes intelligent use of the earth's resources
through research and communication.
Publications, reports, and films.

Friends of the Earth
530 Seventh St., S.E.
Washington, D.C. 20003

An environmental pressure group that campaigns
for conservation, environmental improvement,
and a wise use of resources. Booklets and
pamphlets are available.

Friends of the Earth Foundation
530 Seventh St., S.E.
Washington, D.C. 20003

Dedicated to education, research, litigation, and
publishing for the preservation, restoration, and
rational use of the earth's resources.

Greenpeace U.S.A.
1611 Connecticut Ave., N.W.
Washington, D.C. 20009

Initiates active measures to aid endangered species. Monitors conditions of environmental concerns including ocean dumping, acid rain, and test bannings on nuclear weapons.

Izaak Walton League of America
1401 Wilson Blvd., Level B
Arlington, Va. 22209

Works to educate the public on conserving, protecting, maintaining, and restoring the soil, forest, water, and other natural resources.

Sierra Club
730 Polk Street
San Francisco, Calif. 94109

Publishes a regular newsletter with details of environmental legislation in the United States.

World Nature Association
PO Box 673, Woodmoor Station
Silver Spring, Md. 20901

Naturalists — professional and amateur — interested in conservation and travel. Offers annual scholarship to an American educator in the natural sciences, grants for small research projects, conducts tours. Publications.

Picture Acknowledgments

The publishers would like to thank the following for allowing their photographs to be reproduced in this book: John Baines 23 below, 28; Bruce Coleman Limited 4 (Wayne Lankinen), 5 above (John Shaw), inset (Kim Taylor), 6 (John Brownlie), 8 above (Steve Kaufman), 11 (George McCarthy), 12 (Colin Molyneux), 15 (P A Hinchliffe), 18 (John Shaw), 21 (Hans Reinhard), 23 above, 24 above (Adrian Davies), below (Normal Tomalin), 25 (N Schwartz), 34 (Norman Owen), 40 (Colin Molyneux);CEGB/DIPA Photo Library 32; Greenpeace 36; ICCE 22 (Rod Redknapp) 35 above (Mark Boulton); Andre Maslennikov/IBL Sweden 16, 27; Oxford Scientific Films 14 (GA MaClean), 29 (Steve Littlewood); Rex Features 37 (Boccon); Science Photo Library 30 above (Gazuit); Topham Picture Library 41; ZEFA 8 below, 10 (Hunter), 17 (Adam), 19, 20 (Mosler), 26 (M Becker), 30 below (T Braise), 31 (Bramaz), 33 (Hunter), 35 below (H Schmidt), 38 (G Juckes), 42. The illustrations are by Jane Pickering 18, 22; Malcolm Walker 7; and Brian Watson 6, 9, 13, 15, 21.

Index